I0815595

Rottweilers

by Julie Murray

Abdo Kids Jumbo is an Imprint of Abdo Kids
abdobooks.com

abdobooks.com

Published by Abdo Kids, a division of ABDO, P.O. Box 398166, Minneapolis, Minnesota 55439.

Printed in the United States of America, North Mankato, Minnesota.

102025

012026

Photo Credits: AdobeStock, Alamy, Shutterstock, Thinkstock

Production Contributors: Teddy Borth, Jennie Forsberg, Grace Hansen
Design Contributors: Candice Keimig, Julia Line

Library of Congress Control Number: 2025936495

Publisher's Cataloging-in-Publication Data

Names: Murray, Julie, author.

Title: Rottweilers / by Julie Murray

Description: Minneapolis, Minnesota : Abdo Kids, 2026 | Series: Dogs | Includes online resources and index.

Identifiers: ISBN 9798384907534 (lib. bdg.) | ISBN 9798384908234 (ebook) | ISBN 9798384908586 (read-to-me ebook)

Subjects: LCSH: Rottweiler dog--Juvenile literature. | Livestock protection dogs--Juvenile literature. | Working dogs--Juvenile literature. | Dogs--Juvenile literature. | Dogs--Behavior--Juvenile literature. | Animal behavior--Juvenile literature.

Classification: DDC 636.7--dc23

Table of Contents

Rottweiler

Rottweilers are strong, athletic dogs. They have protective **instincts** that can make them good guard dogs.

The **breed** was brought to the United States in 1930. The dogs came from Germany where they helped **herd** and guard **livestock**. They were also used to pull heavy carts.

Germany
Europe
Africa
N
E
S
W

Rottweilers have big, strong bodies. They can stand 27 inches (68.6 cm) tall and weigh up to 135 pounds (61 kg). Females are smaller than males.

Their coat is short, black, and has rust-colored markings. The dogs have a large head and brown eyes. Their ears flop forward.

Grooming

Rottweilers shed a lot, so grooming them is important. Weekly brushing and an occasional bath will keep their coat clean and healthy. They also need their nails clipped and teeth brushed regularly.

Exercise

Daily exercise is a must for Rottweilers! They like to stay active with long walks and playing fetch.

Rottweilers are working dogs and like having a job to do. They enjoy training exercises. They do well in **obedience** and **tracking** competitions.

Personality

Rottweilers are smart and loyal dogs. They love being with their family! They are **wary** of strangers and protective of their humans.

Rottweilers need proper training. They should also spend time with humans and other dogs from an early age. With this, they can be loving members of the family.

More Facts

- Rottweilers have a strong bite! Their bite force is about half as powerful as a great white shark.
- Their average lifespan is 8 to 10 years.
- The American Kennel Club officially recognized the **breed** in 1931.

Glossary

breed – a particular type of animal.

herd – to gather, lead, or drive a group of animals.

instinct – a natural ability or need to do something.

livestock – cows, horses, sheep, or other animals raised or kept on a farm or ranch.

obedience – having to do with the act of obeying.

tracking – having to do with following a scent trail.

wary – on guard against threat or danger.

Index

Visit **abdokids.com** to access crafts, games, videos, and more!

Use Abdo Kids code **DRK7534** or scan this QR code!